HOLD YOUR HORSES

Horse Idioms, Expressions, and other Memes

BROUGHT TO YOU BY

EQUINE HERITAGE INSTITUTE

The books created by Equine Heritage Institute are designed to preserve the history and majesty of the horse. Our goal is to find, understand, and pass on the valuable data about equine use and its influence on humanity. The Equine Heritage Institute is a not for profit 503(c) and 100% of all proceeds from the sale of books, services, and products support Equine Heritage Institute's mission.

To make a donation to EHI, please visit www.ehi-donations.com

SPECIAL THANKS TO OUR TEAM

Mary Chris Foxworthy, Research Writer

Mary Chris' grandfather owned one of the last creameries in the United States that still used horse-drawn milk wagons. This sparked her life-long love affair with horses and passion for keeping horse history alive. After graduating from college with a degree in Food Science and Communications, Mary Chris bought her very first horse with her first paycheck. Since then, she has served on the board of various equine associations and held a judge's card in Carriage Driving. She is known for her work in the Gloria Austin Collection, and has published and presented numerous equine educational programs. She has written for several equine publications and won an award from American Horse Publications for one of her articles. Mary Chris is an active exhibitor in Carriage Driving and Dressage. Along with her husband, she enjoys spending time with their horses (two Morgans and a PRE), a bouncing Bearded Collie and two adult children and one grandchild.

Abby David, Graphic Designer and Illustrator

Abby David's family has roots in the Walking Horse tradition and she grew up hearing tales of Ole Tobe and Pete the mule's antics, holiday wagon decorations, and trick riding. In her teens she spent her summers boarding the neighbors horses and playing at barrel racing in the back paddock with Thunder. She landed a job as a Graphic Designer at The Arts Center of Cannon County in 2004 and has worked in the print and digital mass communications industry continuously. Since marrying into a family in the racehorse business, she has enjoyed exploring a whole new world of horses and wearing big fancy hats. She also enjoys dancing in all it's forms and teaches in her local community.

Gloria Austin's Collection of Books

ENJOY OUR OTHER BOOKS

- The Brewster Story
- Carriage Lamps
- Gloria Austin's Carriage Collection
- A Glossary of Harness Parts
- Equine Elegance
- The Fire Horse
- Horse Basics 101
- The Unsung Heros of World War One

- The Horse, History, and Human Culture
- Horse Symbolism
- Horses of the Americas
- A Drive Through Time: Carriages, Horses, and History
- The Medieval Horse
- Speak Your Horse's Language

- Tea: Steeped in Tradition
- Woman and Horses
- The Golden Carriage and the House of Hapsburg
- Horses and Newport
- A Cookbook for Horse Lovers
- Dance! To Improve Riding and Driving
- Westward Ho!

Brought To You By The Equine Heritage Institute

HOLD YOUR HORSES
Horse Idioms, Expressions, and other Memes
By: Gloria Austin President of Equine Heritage Institute, Inc. (EHI)

First Publish Date 2020
Copyright © 2020 by Equine Heritage Institute, Inc.

Gloria Austin Carriage Collection, LLC; Equine Heritage Institute, Inc.
3024 Marion County Road Weirsdale, FL 32195 Office: (352) 753-2826 Fax: (352) 753-6186

Ordering Information:
Quantity sales: Special discounts are available on quantity purchases by corporations, associations, and others. For details, contact the publisher at the address above.
Printed in the United States of America First Edition
ISBN: 978-1-951895-11-2 Print, 978-1-951895-12-9 E-book

TABLE OF CONTENTS

The Horse

"We have had 6,000 years of history with the domesticated horse and only 100 years with the automobile."
Gloria Austin

4000 BC   3000 BC   2000 BC   1000 BC   0   1000 AD   PRESENT

EQUINE RELATED
IDIOMS AND EXPRESSIONS

Throughout time, the English language has changed. Words like thou and whence, that were used commonly in medieval times, have become archaic.

The meaning of words has changed over time too. In the late thirteenth century, nice meant foolish, ignorant, frivolous or senseless; today it is a compliment.

The derivations of many words also stem from the past. In feudal England, escheat referred to the situation where the tenant of a field died without an heir so then the land became owned by either the crown or the immediate overlord. The escheator was the local official responsible for upholding the king's rights as feudal lord. Mistrust of the king's escheators led the word into its current sense: a cheater is considered a dishonest gamester or a swindler.

In everyday language many concepts are expressed by idioms, such as hit the road, break the ice, bull in a china shop and kid in a candy shop. An idiom is a phrase or expression that typically presents a figurative, non-literal meaning. Many idiomatic expressions were meant literally in their original use, but sometimes, the attribution of the literal meaning changed and the phrase itself grew away from its original roots. Other idioms are deliberately figurative; for example, break a leg.

A significant portion of idioms and expressions used today are derived from horses and the lifestyle surrounding equestrians. Horses are no longer the primary means of transportation so the meanings of these idioms and expressions are lost on most people. Join us on a trip through time as we cover the meanings of horse terms and equine related names as well as the origins of idioms and expressions related to horses.

Hold Your Horses

Across The Board

This phrase has its origin in horse racing. It denotes a bet in which equal amounts are staked on the same horse to win, place or show in a race. It means "applying to all."

Also Ran

This term originated in the late 19th century and was applied to racehorses that did not finish in the first three. When used as an expression it refers to a person who has lost in a race or contest, especially by a large margin.

Back The Wrong Horse

The expression originated from betting on horses in horse racing. It means making a wrong choice or to support someone or something that will not succeed.

Beat A Dead Horse

In the mid 19th century they used to beat a horse to make it go faster. (This practice is unacceptable today.)It would be pointless to beat a dead horse as it would not go anywhere. Today this expression means wasting energy on a lost cause or an unalterable situation.

Farmer John Shreiner and his Conestoga Wagon,
Lancaster County, PA, circa 1910.

Be There With Bells On

In the days of delivering freight by horse or mule
drawn wagons, the teamsters would often festoon
their horses with ornate bells. If they became stuck
or otherwise needed help from another teamster,
they had to pay the one helping them get out of
trouble by giving him some of their bells. Therefore,
if you arrived at your destination without the help of
anyone else, or perhaps even gave aid along the way,
you arrived "with bells on."

To Bridle One's Tongue

A bridle for a horse includes both the headstall that
holds a bit that goes in the mouth of a horse and
the reins that are attached to the bit. When riding a
horse, the bridle is used for control. To "bridle one's
tongue" is to control what is said in order to conform
to civil language.

Buck Like A Bronco

A bucking bronco commonly refers to an untrained horse that behaves unpredictably, usually by kicking or bucking. The expression "buck like a bronco" refers to someone who is hard to teach or train.

Done In A Canter

The canter is a three beat, easy going gait of the horse. The pilgrims, on their way to the tomb of Thomas a' Becket in Canterbury, often rode at this speed giving this gait its name. "Done in a canter" means to accomplish something with ease or minimal effort.

Champ At The Bit

This mid-1600s expression refers to the action of a horse that impatiently bites the bit in its mouth. Today it means to show impatience at being held back or delayed.

Charley Horse

The origin of this term may relate to an old workhorse that was tasked with pulling a roller across a baseball infield. Often in the 1800s, old workhorses kept on the grounds of ballparks were called Charley. The movements of the injured, stiff-legged ballplayers were likened to the labored plodding of these old horses, and the injury itself eventually became known as a "Charley horse".

Curry Favor

The expression derives from the currying (grooming) of a mythical French horse called Fauvel. In the poem, the rich and powerful humiliate themselves by bowing down and stroking the coat of Fauvel. The expression means to seek or advance oneself through fl attery or fawning.

Dark Horse

This expression goes back to 1831. Prime Minister Benjamin Disraeli wrote a novel called, *The Young Duke.* In the book, there is a description of a horse race in which the two favorites are not running well in a race. An unknown, dark colored horse ends up winning. A person whose qualities are little known, although they may have recently had success or are about to have success, is called a "dark horse".

Dead Heat

The term "dead heat" comes from horse-racing. Heat used to mean simply a race. The term was in use by the late eighteenth century and often seen in publications: "The whole race was run head and head, terminating in a dead heat." *Sporting Magazine*, 1796. Today it is applied to any contest in which there is a tie.

Dead Ringer

A dead ringer is a person or thing that seems exactly like someone or something else. In the past unscrupulous racehorse owners who had a fast horse and a slow horse that were nearly identical in appearance, would run the slow horse until the betting odds reached the desired level, then they substituted the "ringer" who could run much faster. Dead in this case means abrupt or exact, like in dead stop.

Die in Harness

"Die in harness" is a reference to when armies rode horses to war. A member of the military who dies while still in service dies "in harness". It is a way of saying the person was working up until his death. Since horses are thought of as noble creatures, it is a way of honoring a person. The term is used in other professions as well.

Donkey's Years

This expression comes from the parallel between a long time and saying that something is as long as donkey's ears. A slurring of pronunciation resulted in the present form or from the British rhyming slang, replacing years with ears. It has come to mean a long while or a lengthy period.

14

Don't look a gift horse in the mouth

Horses have gum lines that recede with age. Hence older horses have longer teeth than younger horses. A horse's age is determined by examining the horse's mouth closely and therefore its usefulness and/or worth. "Looking a gift horse in the mouth" means to immediately judge a gift based on its worth or usefulness rather than the thought behind it. It is considered rude, and ungrateful since one is finding fault with something that has been received as a gift or favor.

Down to the wire

This phrase refers to races where the winner is determined by whoever first crosses the finish line which was a string stretched across to help the judges see clearly who crosses first in a close race. That string, called the wire or tape, determined the winner by who broke it first. Hence "down to the wire" means undecided until the last minute.

Eat like a horse

This term refers to eating large quantities of food or someone with a large appetite. The idiom alludes to the idea that horses eat a lot. They seem to eat constantly and will eat whatever is available.

Feeling His Oats

When horses eat oats, they are more energetic so this expression refers to feeling energetic or frisky or to act boldly.

Find The Pony

The origin of the phrase is from a story of two brothers, one optimistic and one pessimistic. Their parents were worried about what gift to give the pessimistic son as he could not be easily pleased. After several ideas and considerations they bought him a bicycle. Unfortunately they had little time for the optimistic son and put some horse droppings in a box and gift wrapped it. Predictably, the pessimistic son was unhappy with the bicycle being certain he would fall and injure himself. When the optimistic son opened his box, he exclaimed, "there must be a pony in here somewhere!" The phrase means to find value or good where none is evident. There must be a pony in here somewhere was one of Ronald Reagan's favorite stories.

For The Birds

Before the advent of cars, one could see and smell the manure from horses that were pulling carriages and delivery wagons in large cities. Since there was no way of controlling the manure, it served to nourish a large population of birds. If you said that something was "for the birds", you were politely saying that it is load of "crap".

For the Birds

Just doing my part.

Gentle As A Horse

Horses are not aggressive. They are gentle with people. Saying "gentle as a horse" means to be considerate or kindly in disposition, amiable and tender, not harsh or severe.

Get A Leg Up

"Getting a leg up" is from the act of an equestrian receiving help in mounting a horse. The helper would create a foothold by cupping the hands to heft the rider upward, throwing a leg up and over the steed. The expression means to get a boost or advantage.

Get Off My Back

When a carriage arrived at a destination, a carpet was rolled out over the mud. If the carpet was too short, the servant would lay, face down, so the passengers could step on his back without getting muddy. The phrase "get off my back" is an expression that means "stop annoying me."

Get One's Goat

Hyperactive racehorses were often given goats as stable mates because their presence tended to have a calming effect on the horses. After the horse became attached to the goat, it got very upset when its companion disappeared - making it run poorly on the track. In the 19th century, when a devious gambler wanted a horse to lose, he would get the horse's goat and take it away the night before the race, thus agitating the horse. "Get one's goat" means to irritate someone.

Head Up And Tail Over The Dashboard

When a horse has its head up and its tail over the carriage dashboard, it's feeling very perky. The saying is meant to describe something that is going very well.

Hell Bent For Leather

"Hell bent" means to be highly or stubbornly determined. "Hell for leather" is more literal. In this case leather refers to the bridle and saddle on a horse. To ride in a harsh manner is rough on the bridle, stirrup leathers and saddle and is literally "hell for leather". "Hell bent for leather" then is to ride very fast and very determined. The idiom means to go all out and to be willing to do whatever it takes to achieve an objective.

High Horse

This expression alludes to the use of tall horses by high-ranking persons and dates from the late 1700s. "Get off your high horse" is telling someone to act less arrogantly and more humbly.

Hitch In Our Plan

The word "hitch" comes from the Scottish. It means that the motion is jerky. If a horse has a slight limp it is sometimes called a hitch. If the horse develops a hitch en route to a destination, horse and rider will most likely not arrive on time and thus there's a "hitch in our plan".

Hobson's Choice

This expression dates back to 1631 to a man named Hobson who ran a livery stable in Cambridge. He was well known in his day. He was renowned for the fact he would only let out his horses in strict rotation - there was no choice at all. The term means "no choice at all".

Hold Your Horses

"Hold your horses" literally means to keep your horses still. Using the expression means to tell someone to wait, to relax, to slow down, to be patient or to be more careful before acting.

Hoof It

The hoof is the foot of the horse. To "hoof it" means to travel on foot. In 1920s American slang, a dancer was called a hoofer.

Horse Around

Horses play with each other physically. It is usually very fast and often very rough. It can involve running, biting, kicking, rearing and striking. Usually, no horse gets seriously hurt. "Horsing around" is rough or rowdy play, usually in good fun.

Horse Of A Different Color

Horses are registered at birth and the registration includes a record of their color. Horses sometimes change color as they age so the registration may not match the actual color of the horse leading one to suspect the horse is not the one in the registration. The term is used to point out a difference rather than likeness.

Horsefeathers

Billy de Beck was the author of the popular cartoon Barney Google, which frequently featured dialogue with a horse - his sidekick Spark Plug. He also created a short cartoon film called Horsefeathers, which appeared in US cinemas in 1928. The term was used to express disdain or disbelief.

Horse Neck

The "Horse's Neck" is a drink that falls within the cooler category. It is made with whiskey and ginger ale. The drink—which gets its name from its long, loopy lemon twist garnish that curls along inside of the glass—is one of several classic drinks that devolved into a mocktail around Prohibition

Horselaugh

A neigh is the high-pitched sound uttered by a horse. A horselaugh refers to a laugh that is loud and boisterous resembling a horse's neigh.

Horseplay

The origin of "horseplay" dates back to the 1580's. In the 16th century, "horse" was an adjective describing anything strong, big or coarse. Horseplay meant strong play.

Horse - Plant Name

The horse was important in medieval England, where present-day English was largely formed. It's not surprising then that we now have numerous expressions that refer to horses. These usually allude to the hefty and coarse working horses of the Middle Ages. This is apparent in the way that rural language was formed. Any plant that resembled another but was large and coarser would be known as horse-'plant name of choice': Horse-daisy (country name for the Ox-eye Daisy) Horse-radish (a large root resembling a radish but with a fiery taste) Horse-gentian (a.k.a. Feverwort) Horse-nettle (Nightshade) Horse-parsley (Alexanders - an outsize parsley-like plant tasting of celery)

Horse Sense

In 1870 the New York magazine, The Nation, offered a corroborative view of the expression's origin: "The new phrase - born in the West, we believe - of 'horsesense', which is applied to the intellectual ability of men who exceed others in practical wisdom."

Hoss

Hoss refers to a person who is dependable and strong as a horse. Who remembers Hoss Cartwright from Bonanza?

Horse Plant

Ox-eye Daisy

Ox-eye Daisy Horse

Inside Track

Wait, what? And now we have two horses running neck and neck. Both are on the inside track. If that is even possible.

Finally I got the inside track.

In The Cart

This expression means "in trouble" and originated from the practice of taking prisoners for execution in horsedrawn carts. Victims were transported to the gallows in a cart, the noose was attached to the victim's neck and then the cart was driven away.

In The Pink

In the pink means in good health. Fox hunters wear scarlet jackets called hunting "pinks"; derived from a tailor named Thomas Pink. "'In the pink'" refers to both the jackets and to the healthy, energetic approach to the pastime that many fox hunters adopt.

Inside Track

The best position for a horse in a race is the one nearest the rail - the "inside track". The expression means to be in an advantageous position.

Jump On The Bandwagon

Many decades ago candidates for political offices often rode through town in horse-drawn wagons on which a band was playing music to attract a crowd. If the candidate was popular, people would jump onto his bandwagon to show their support. Today "jump on the bandwagon" has come to mean to follow the trend.

Kick Over The Traces

Traces are straps that attach from the horse's driving collar to the object it is pulling. If the horse kicks over the traces, it steps over these leather straps making it impossible for the driver to control the animal. The term "kick over the traces" has come to mean insubordination or to be reckless or unruly.

Kick Like A Mule

Mules are known to have a strong kick. "Kick like a mule" means to have a strong effect. For example: "This drink tastes horrible but it kicks like a mule!"

Lock The Stable Door After The Horse Has Bolted

If you say that someone has closed or shut the stable door after the horse has bolted, you mean that they have tried to prevent something from happening but they have done so too late to prevent damage being done.

Long In The Tooth

A horse's age is determined by it's teeth. Their gums recede with age, making their teeth long, and their occulssion angle gets steeper with age. The longer the teeth, the older the horse. So saying someone is "long in the tooth" means they are old.

Wait, What? You are how old?

Long In The Tooth

Neck and Neck

Rolling in manure won't make a stallion outta you but, it will make the stallion in you smell better.

Stallion

Mare's Nest

Mares don't make nests, hence the confusion that arises in looking for one. Saying that something is a "mare's nest" means that it is a place, condition or situation of great disorder or confusion.

Mulish

Poorly trained mules are said to be stubborn. Saying someone is mulish means that they are stubborn and not open minded.

Neck and Neck

The origin of this phrase is from horse racing, where two or more horses that are evenly matched might run closely together towards the finish line, side by side. When this happens, the horses are said to be "neck and neck". The expression refers to two people or things that are so close or similar that it's impossible to tell which is better or winning.

On the wagon

Water wagons were a commonplace sight in US cities many years ago. They did not carry drinking water but were used to dampen down dusty streets during dry weather. Those who had quit drinking and were tempted to lapse said that they would drink from the water wagon rather than take to drinking so the term "on the wagon" came to mean abstaining from drinking alcoholic beverages.

Piss Like A Racehorse

"Piss like a horse" means to urinate a massive amount. When there is urgency, the word "racehorse" is added.

Prance Like A Horse

When you run up on stage to accept an award you may move in such an excited way as to prance. The definition of a horse moving this way is the original meaning of prance and it probably comes from the Middle English pranken, "to show off ."

Put The Cart Before The Horse

Everyone knows that the cart goes behind the horse! To "put the cart before the horse" means to do things in the wrong order, rendering it ineffective.

Putting The Saddle On The Wrong Horse

"Putting the saddle on the wrong horse" means to place blame on an innocent person or to give credit for something to the wrong person.

Riding For A Fall

This phrase originated as a late 19th-century and meant to ride a horse, especially in the hunting field, in such a way as to make an accident likely. When it is used as an expression it means that something is likely to fail.

Put The Cart Before The Horse

Onward!

Run Like A Quarter

A quarter horse is a small, strong horse that can run very fast for short distances. It's not intended for long trips. To say that someone "runs like a quarter horse" means that they do the first part of something well.

Run For The Money

The literal origin of the phrase comes from horse racing. To want a "run for your money" is to want a horse that you have placed a bet on to run well in the race. To have a run for one's money is to have a good determined struggle for something.

Saddle Idioms

Tall in the saddle: To act or conduct oneself in a manner that is imposing, impressive, resolute or manly.

Back in the saddle: Resuming something after an absence.

In the saddle: To be in control of a situation; to be in a position of power.

Saddle with: To force one to deal with someone or something that proves to be a great burden.

Burr under the saddle: Someone or something that is a constant cause of trouble or annoyance.

Saddle on a sow: Something that looks completely ridiculous, abnormal, or out of place.

Saddle up: To put a saddle on a horse, to get ready to do something.

Sick As A Horse, Healthy As A Horse

When a person has nausea unrelieved by vomiting, they are said to be "sick as a horse". Since a horse is unable to vomit, the nausea of a horse is more lasting and more violent. Conversely, a horse is seen as a symbol of strength and physical capacity so "healthy as a horse" means someone is feeling great.

Straight From The Horse's Mouth

This saying derives from a boast of confidence from a racetrack tipster who says he gets his information from the horses themselves. "Straight from the horse's mouth" means that the information is directly from a reputable source.

Stick A Pony In Me Pocket

The phrase appears in the opening song of the British TV series Only Fools and Horses. The words of the song mean, slip me some money on the sly and I'll go get the goods. The characters in the show specialize in shady deals. The words of the song are:

Stick a pony in me pocket,

I'll fetch the suitcase from the van,

Cause if you want the best 'uns,

And you don't ask questions,

Then brother I'am your man…

Stubborn As A Mule

Mules have a sometimes undeserved reputation for obstinacy so to say someone is "stubborn as a mule" means they are obstinate.

That's A Horse On Me

The expression refers to an unexpected turn of fortune or a joke at someone's expense. The first cite is from Eugene Field's 1889 A Little Book of Western Verse (p. 101), in the poem, "Mr. Dana of the New York Sun"

Take The Bit

This expression alludes to a horse biting on the bit and taking control away from the rider. To "take the bit" means to take charge or to begin doing something with decisive, independent resolve.

Don't Change Horses In Midstream

The saying is credited to Abraham Lincoln. Lincoln used the phrase "no time to swap horses" when talking about the presidential election during the Civil War, as well as talking about replacing his generals. The expression means that one should not change plans in the middle of the project.

The Horse Is Out Of The Barn

If the horse has escaped out of the barn it will be hard to catch him. The expression "the horse is out of the barn" means that an action is useless since it is too late.

Throw Someone To The Wolves

In the Victorian days, printmakers frequently depicted sleighs drawn by horses at full gallop, being chased by packs of wolves. Allegedly, if the wolves got too close, one of the passengers was thrown out in hopes that the rest of the passengers could escape while the animals devoured the victim. Although no one is sure if this really happened, it resulted in this metaphor to "throw someone to the wolves". The expression means to abandon someone or allow somebody else to be criticized or attacked in order to protect oneself.

Wild Goose Chase

In the 1500s, there was a popular type of horse race where riders had to follow a lead rider through an unpredictable course. This reminded many people of flying geese in formation following a leader, so the sport was called a "wild-goose chase". The expression means that something is a foolish and hopeless pursuit of something unattainable.

Is this a wild horse chase or a wild goose chase?

WILD GOOSE CHASE

Win Hands Down

A jockey needs to keep a tight rein in order to encourage their horse to run. If someone is very far ahead, he can afford to slacken off and still win even if he drops his hands and loosens the reins. Hence to "win hands down" means to win by an enormous margin.

Work Like A Horse

Horses have evolved by natural selection to have thick muscles, a large heart and powerful lungs. Strength is part of their makeup. Hence the phrases, "strong as a horse", and "work like a horse".

You Can Lead A Horse To Water But Can't Make Him Drink

After a long ride a rider will typically lead their horse to water to take a drink. It is well known that many times the horse will not drink. The expression means you can give someone an opportunity but not force them to take it.

TERMINOLOGY OF THE 19TH CENTURY
GOLDEN AGE OF COACHING

My vehicle's engine has a mind of his own with no brake pedal.

Give me some space.

"We'll arrange for your driver's license to be mailed by express post, it will get to you tomorrow", they said.

Now I'm stuck driving the only thing that doesn't requre a driver's licence.

A Long Set - Two cockhorses

Artist - A great coachman

Benjamin - A greatcoat worn by a coachman also called Inverness cape or Carrick coat.

Both Sides Of The Road - A team worked up and back a stage the same day - sometimes called two sweats.

Boot - Projections at the side or rear of the coach.

Chapman - A trader

Cockhorse - An additional horse to assist the team on steep hills - ridden postilion.

Crab – the end of the pole

Cross Team - Two grays and two darker horses.

"Feather edging it"- Driving very close to another carriage.

Gamon Seat - The second seat on a coach - A back gamon is the rear-facing seat on coach roof.

Hackney Man - a man who rented horses.

Handling The Ribbons - The manipulation of the reins.

Jobmaster - The person that hired out horses, harness and vehicles and either carried on business at a coach office or at an inn.

Leaders - Front pair of four or six horses.

Light Horse - A gray or horse with white markings driven as a lead horse to be seen at night.

Mail Coach - called "The Mail".

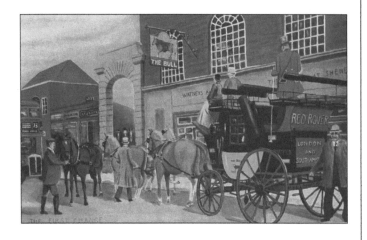

People who say carriage driving isn't a sport are just intimidated....

because in OUR game the ball has a mind of its own!

Only two emotions should be in the driver's seat: patience and a sense of humor.

Mail Receiving Office - The country inn which received letters.

Putting to - Harnessing and hitching the horses

Springing The Team - To put the horses in a canter at the bottom of a steep hill.

Stagecoach - Public coach running over an advertised route with names like Rocket and Telegraph.

Stage - The distance between one change of horse and another.

Swing - Middle pair of six horses.

Wheelers - Rear pair of four or six horses.

EQUINE TERMINOLOGY

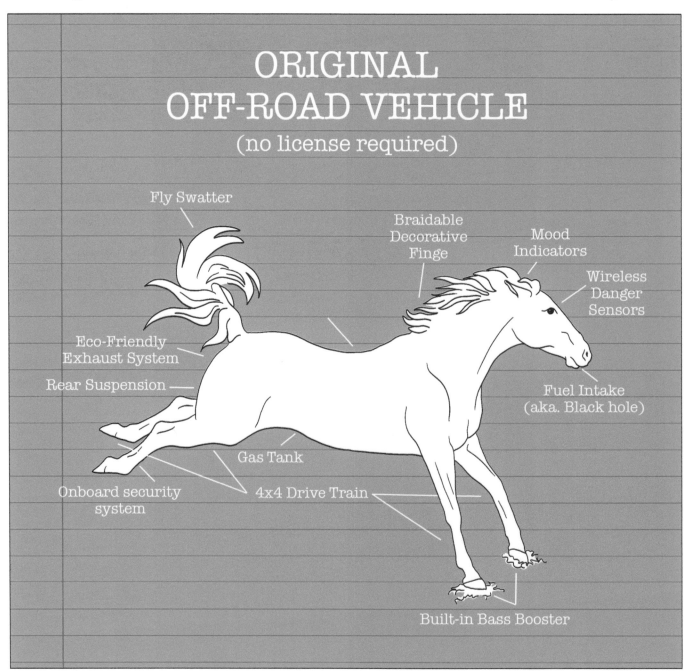

ORIGINAL
OFF-ROAD VEHICLE
(no license required)

Fly Swatter

Braidable Decorative Finge

Mood Indicators

Wireless Danger Sensors

Eco-Friendly Exhaust System

Rear Suspension

Fuel Intake (a.k.a. Black hole)

Gas Tank

Onboard security system

4x4 Drive Train

Built-in Bass Booster

Ace or ACP
Slang term for the drug acepromazine or acetyl promazine (trade names Atravet or Acezine) - The drug is a sedative.

Action
This term refers to the movement of the horse, usually relative to a specific gait and related anatomical functions required to achieve that gait.

Aged Horse
Recent research has defined the "aged" or "geriatric" horse as 15 years or over and a horse as very old if it is 30 years of age or older.

Aging
Technique used to estimate a horse's age by inspecting its teeth

Aids
Refers to communication devices used to communicate instructions to the horse - Common aids are either natural, such as hands, seat, weight, legs and vocal commands or artificial aids which include bits, whips, spurs and martingales.

Airs Above The Ground
The airs above the ground ,or school jumps, are a series of higher-level, haute ecole, classical dressage movements in which the horse leaves the ground.

Amateur
An uncompensated exhibitor of horses

Amble
A gait, specific to certain breeds of horses, generally more smooth than a trot, with a specific foot positioning and timing

Ankle
While sometimes the fetlock is colloquially referred to as an "ankle", that terminology is not correct. The fetlock is a metacarpophalangeal joint which corresponds to the human upper knuckle, such as that on the ball of the foot.

Arena
Any enclosed area designated for training or riding horses.

Artificial Insemination
A breeding technique which refers to the human assisted insemination using various methods that do not involve the mare and stallion interacting directly.

Average Earnings Index (AEI)
The average earnings index measures the earning power of a stallion or mare's off spring by comparing the average earnings of a given horse's progeny with all other runners of the same age that raced in the same country in a given period of time.

Behaves like
a saint
in warm-up

Enters the
Arena
in Feral Mode

Did you say, "Whoa?"

I'm pretty darned sure you said, "Whoa."

Balk, Balking
The term refers to a horse refusing to move on command.

Barefoot or Unshod
A horse without shoes

Bearing Rein, Overcheck or Check Rein
A strap used to prevent the horse from lowering its head beyond a fixed point.

Bearing Rein

Bell Boot
A protective boot.

Billet
A billet strap is a piece of leather or nylon located on either side of a saddle and used to hold the girth in place. English saddles commonly have billet straps on both sides whereas a western saddle will have a single "off-billet" strap on the off side and a latigo strap on the near side.

Bell Boot

Bit
Any device placed into the mouth of a horse and used to direct and guide the animal.

Black Points
Markings on a horse - black mane, tail, legs and ear rims.

Black Type
Black type face is used to distinguish horses that have won or placed in an approved stake race - winners receive upper case black type; second and third placed finishers have lower case black type.

Bloodhorse
Refers to horse breeding - especially Thoroughbred horse breeding.

Blowing
Refers to the sound made by a horse by sharply exhaling through fl ared nostrils. This sound is considered shorter than a snort.

Bolting
Uncontrolled, sudden movement of a horse.

Botfly, Bot
A parasitic fly that lays its eggs on the legs, muzzle, and jaw of horses.

Bowed, Tendon
An enlarged tendon specific to the cannon bones, most commonly associated with heavy work

I never fall off. I just dismount with style!

Branding
Technique used to identify an animal by burning the skin.

Breeching Strap
A strap around the rear of a horse. Both under saddle and in harness - Breeching engages when an animal slows down or travels downhill; it is used to brake or stabilize a load.

Breeder
Horse breeders evaluate animals, direct breeding procedures and oversee the general care of horses.

Breeding
"The breeding" refers to the pedigree of an animal. "Breeding" is the mating and production of off spring.

Bridle
The equipment used on the head of a horse which holds the bit in a horse's mouth and includes the reins.

Bronc Or Bronco
Depending on context, either an unbroken feral horse or a horse used in rodeo bronc riding events.

When Non-Horsey people help out at the barn.

Broodmare
A female horse used for breeding.

Brothers-in-Blood
Those horses who are sired by the same horse or out of full sisters or out of the same dam and sired by full brothers.

Bucking
A behavior where the horse lowers its head and rapidly kicks its hind feet into the air.

Bumper Pull
Refers to a horse trailer pulled by a hitch that is attached to the frame of the towing vehicle near the bumper.

Bute
Nickname for Phenylbutazone, a non-steroid anti-inflammatory drug (NSAID) used to control pain and swelling in horses.

By
In breeding, the relationship of a horse to its sire.

Cannon Or Cannon Bone
A large bone which provides the major support of the horse's weight.

Horses are one of the best reasons to wake up early.

And then the Announcer called for Canter

Canner
A horse of poor quality, referencing animals destined for slaughter.

Canter
A gait, consisting of a three-beat motion.

Caparison
A caparison is a cloth covering laid over a horse or other animal for protection and decoration.

Carriage
A two or four-wheeled vehicle drawn by horses, and used as a conveyance.

Cart
A two-wheeled vehicle pulled by one or more animals.

Cast
A horse is said to be cast when he is laying down in such a manner as to position himself with his legs so close to a wall or fence that he can neither get up nor reposition himself to roll the other way.

Castration
Neutering of a male horse.

And that kids, is why you always check your cinch!

Chef d'equipe
Equestrian team manager, refers most often to state, national or international level.

Chestnut
As related to color of a horse: Reddish-brown coat color. Also: Chestnuts appear on the front legs of a horse above the knee, or sometimes on the back legs of a horse below the hock; thought to be vestigial toes of Eohippus, an early ancestor of the modern horse that lived 50 million years ago.

Choke
Esophageal blockage.

Chrome
Common use term for eye-catching white markings on a horse, like stockings or socks.

Cinch
A girth is sometimes called a cinch on Western saddles. It is a piece of equipment used to keep the saddle in place on a horse or other animal. It passes under the barrel of the equine and attaches to the saddle on both sides.

Calico
A horse with a pinto pattern, generally referring to a sabino-type pattern.

Just finished clipping my horse!

Clipping
Refers to trimming hair in a horse.

Cross
The Bible tells us that a donkey carried Jesus into Jerusalem on Palm Sunday. Legend says that the shadow of the cross fell upon the shoulders and back of the donkey.

Coach
A large heavy vehicle designed to carry passengers.

Coach House Or Carriage House
A building used to keep private carriages.

Cob
Not a breed but rather a type of horse usually of a stout build, with strong bones, large joints, and steady disposition.

Cold-blood
Refers to group of equines known for their strength, stamina and steady temperament - Examples of cold blooded horses include the Clydesdale, the Shire and the Belgian.

Colic
Refers to a broad range of digestive disorders characterized by intestinal displacement or blockage.

Colt
Ungelded young male horse - In most breeds a colt is under three years of age.

Combined Driving
Equestrian sport involving carriage driving - designed to test a driver's ability and the horse(s)' obedience, speed and athleticism, in three demanding phases.

Conformation
Proportional structure of a horse relative to standards for the breed.

Coronary Band
The coronary band, also called coronet, is the junction between hoof wall and hairline.

Counter Canter
A canter in which the horse is required to canter with the outside leg leading, which is opposite of usual.

Coupling
The area where the back and loins join the croup.

You know that tingly feeling you get when horse shopping?

That is common sense leaving your body.

Covering

To breed a mare - "live cover": the mare is brought to the stallion's residence and is covered "live" - "artifi cial Insemination" (AI): the mare is inseminated by a veterinarian.

Cribbing

Involves a horse grasping a solid object such as the stall door or fence rail with its incisor teeth, arching its neck, and contracting the lower neck muscles to retract the larynx caudally.

Crop

A stiff , short-handled whip.

Crossbred

Any horse that is a cross between two known breeds.

Croup

That area running from the tail to the loin, including the underlying musculature of the hindquarters.

Crowhop

A stiff -legged hop with a rounding of the back and absent of a kick.

Crownpiece

The portion of a bridle which goes behind the horse's ears.

Your Horse Only Crowhopped

Stop telling everybody that you can ride the buck out of one.

Curb or Curb Bit
A type of bit that has shanks for leverage.

Curb
Collection of soft tissue injuries of the distal plantar hock region (the long band of tissue that runs down the lower part of the back of the hock).

Daisy Cutter
Horse that moves with long but low movement.

Dam
Female parent of a horse.

Damsire
The sire (father) of a dam (mother); equivalent to a maternal grandfather.

Dapples
Circles of slightly diff erent shade than the rest of the coat.

Distaff
Races limited to female horses are referred to as distaff races.

What did the mother horse say to her foal?

It's pasture your bedtime.

Dock

The tail of the horse and other equines consists of two parts, the dock and the skirt. The dock consists of the muscles and skin covering the coccygeal vertebrae. The term "skirt" refers to the long hairs that fall below the dock.

Docking

Practice of cutting a horse's tail at the dock

Hostler's Toe

Hostler - a person who takes care of horses at an inn, stable, etc.; a groom. Hostler's toe - An injury afflicted to the hostler by the horse stepping on the hostler's toe.

Domestic Horse

There is only one species of domestic horse, but around 400 different breeds. While most horses are domestic, there are some that remain wild. Feral horses are the descendants of once-tame animals that have run free for generations.

Doping

Illegal use of enhancements, chemical or herbal to change performance.

Double-Bank

Jumps that are steps up or down from one level to another and can be single jumps or built as a "staircase" of double or multiple banks.

It was nice of you to spend so much time grooming me

I think it helped to get the mud to stick to me better.

Draft or Draught Horse

Any breed of large, muscular, heavy horses used primarily for plowing fields, pulling wagons, logging and similar work.

Dressage

French word evolved from the verb dresseur meaning "to train" - an equine sport based on classical principles of horsemanship.

Drift

Term for the gathering/round up of feral ponies.

Driving

Controlling one or more horses from behind with some form of horse-drawn vehicle attached.

English Riding

The style of riding using a flat saddle; the bridle usually has a cavesson-style noseband, with reins carried in both hands and generally used with steady contact with the horse's mouth.

Equestrian

An individual familiar with horses and horse handling.

Equine

Any member of the genus Equus.

Ride a Draft Horse . . . . . . it will make your butt look smaller.

Tells you her horse will never kick.

Horse almost kicks your head off. She blames you.

Equitation
The art or practice of horse riding or horsemanship - more specifically refers to a rider's position while mounted and encompasses a rider's ability to ride correctly.

Equus
The genus including the horse, donkey, zebra and all other surviving members of the Equidae family.

Ergot
Found on the back of a horse's fetlock on all four legs - thought to be a vestigial sole pad of ancestral multi-toed equidae.

False Martingale
Strap of leather designed to keep the breastplate in place by attaching to the center of the girth and onto a fitting on the breastplate.

Farrier
A craftsman who trims and shoes horses' hooves.

Feather
The long hair on the fetlocks of horses.

Federation Equestre Internationale (FEI)
The governing body for most international-levels of equestrian competitions.

Live life like someone left the gate open

Feedbag or Nosebag
A food container which attaches to a horse's head.

Feral Horse
Free roaming horses, often horses erroneously called "wild" horses - actually descended from domesticated horses.

Fetlock
The joint of a horse's leg between the cannon bone and the pastern.

Filly
A young female horse less than four years old.

Flank
The side of a horse.

Flea-Bitten
Gray or roan horse with small spots on a mostly white background.

Flea-Bitten

Float
An equine dental term referring to the rasping down of sharp points that may form on horse teeth.

When you eat out. . . because nothing in the house sounds good.

Foal
A horse of either sex less than one year old.

Foaling or To Foal
Birthing of a horse by a mare.

Foaling Box
A large stall with adequate space and privacy for a mare about to foal.

Foal At Side
A suckling foal running with its dam.

Founder
Very painful condition affecting the feet of horse - known technically as laminitis - occurs when there is inflammation of the laminae.

Foundation Sire
The stallion to which all members of a breed trace.

Four-in-Hand
A team of four horses with all their reins joined in hand allowing one driver to control all of them.

Frog
The rubbery part of the underside of a horse hoof.

Full Board or Full Livery

A livery yard or boarding stable is a place where horse owners keep their horses. Full livery/board means a stall is provided along with turn-out for the horse. Bedding, hay and feed are also included and sometimes exercise.

Full-Brother or Full-Sister

Animals with the same sire and the same dam.

Furlong

An eighth of a mile, 220 yards/200m.

Gallop

Fastest gait of a horse averaging about 25 to 30 miles per hour.

Gait

The pattern and way a horse moves its legs is called the gait.

Gaited Horse

Horse breeds that have selective breeding for natural gaited tendencies - that is, the ability to perform one of the smooth-to-ride, intermediate speed, four-beat horse gaits, collectively referred to as ambling gaits.

Gelding

A castrated male horse.

Why is it hard to talk to a racehorse?

They don't stand around furlong

See ...
I told you the
girth was loose!

Get
The off spring of a stallion.

Girth
Piece of equipment used to keep the saddle in place on a horse or other animal - It passes under the barrel of the equine, usually attached to the saddle on both sides by two or three leather straps called billets.

Glass Eye
A blue eye on a horse.

Glass Eye

Gooseneck
A trailer whose forward part is arched like a goose's neck and swiveled to the motor unit.

Grade
An unregistered horse.

Grand Prix
Highest levels of either show jumping or dressage as governed by the rules of the FEI.

Green
An untrained horse or rider that is just beginning training.

Green-Broke
Refers to horses that have been ridden under saddle a few times.

Groom
A person who is responsible for some or all aspects of the management of horses and/or the care of the stables themselves.

Grooming
The complete care, cleaning and inspection of all parts of a horse.

Groundwork
To work a horse without a rider, controlling it from the ground.

Hack
Commonly refers to one of two things: as a verb, it describes the act of riding a horse for light exercise, and as a noun, it is a type of horse used for riding out at ordinary speeds over roads and trails.

Hackamore
Headgear utilizing a noseband for control instead of a bit.

Half-bred
Having only one parent that is purebred.

Hold onto what makes you happy.

If it tries to buck you off, just hold on even tighter.

Half-Halt
Coordinated action of the seat, the legs and the hand of the rider, with the object of increasing the attention and balance of the horse before the execution of certain actions such as gait changes.

Halter
Headgear designed for leading or tying a horse.

Hand
1 hand = 4 inches, a measurement used in reference to the height of a horse.

Hand Gallop
Refers to a gait faster than a canter but slower than a full gallop.

Hard Keeper
A horse which needs a large amount of food to maintain weight.

Haute Ecole
Haute école ("high school"), refers to the advanced components of classical dressage.

Harness
Horse tack used to hitch a horse to a cart, plow, wagon or other vehicle.

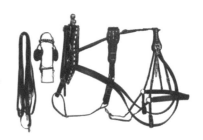

Harness

STANDARDBREDS
Cause who wants to canter?

Harness Racing
Racing horses pulling a single person cart or sulky.

Hayloft
Space above a barn or stable to store hay.

Head-Shy
Any horse that is reluctant to have its head handled.

Headstall
That portion of the bridle which consists of straps that goes over the horse's head and under the throat.

Heavy
Horses that lean on your hands - usually the result of the horse not being taught to yield to the pressure of the bit.

Heavy Hunter
A heavily built hunter type horse often bred by crossing a Thoroughbred with a Draft horse.

Hebdra Virus / Henipavirus
Hendra virus was fi rst described in 1994 after an outbreak of acute respiratory disease in a Thoroughbred training stable in Australia in which horses and one person were fatally infected.

Hinny
A hybrid offspring of a male horse and a female donkey.

Hobbies
Device placed around the legs to prevent a horse from wandering.

Hock
Located on the hind legs just above the cannon bones - functions to carry weight, push off the ground and allow the horse to run, jump, turn, and play.

Horse Blanket
Covering made for horses to cover the animal's body from chest to rump.

Horse Meat
The meat of equines - in antiquity, most nations ate horse meat. Consumption slowly declined when horses became a tool for conquest, leisure and a means of transportation or a work tool.

Horse Latitudes
When Spaniards carried horses aboard their ships to the colonies in the West Indies, many horses died before reaching land. The dead horses were thrown overboard at about 30 degrees north and south of the equator. This location is called the "horse latitudes".

Horse Power

Equivalent to the normal sustained power output of one horse.

Horse Racing

The sport of racing horses.

Horseshoe

A curved bar attached to the underside of the wall of the hoof to prevent wear and provide grip.

Horse Trailer

A trailer designed to carry horses.

Hostler

A groom or stableman, who is employed in a stable to take care of horses, usually at an inn.

Hot-Blood

Hot blood horses are comprised of ancient horse breeds originating from the Middle East. They were mainly bred for speed and agility. Hot bloods are often high -spirited, bold and quick learners.

Hunters

Type of horse showing where the horse and rider jump a course and the judging is based on accuracy, grace and elegance.

In-Hand
Competition where horses are led rather than ridden or driven and judged on conformation and movement.

Intermediate
Mid-levels of dressage competition as governed by the FEI.

Irons or Stirrup Irons
A stirrup iron, in the English riding disciplines, suspends from a narrow strip of leather and offers a fl at base of support for the ball of the rider's foot to assist with mounting and riding. Stirrup irons got their name from centuries' old versions that were originally forged from iron.

Jack
An uncastrated male donkey.

Jockey
The rider of a horse in horse racing.

Jog
A slow trot, considered a Western gait.

Jump
(noun) An obstacle, used in competition or in cross country riding.

IF IT DOESN'T JUMP

THROW IT OVER!

When it's finally windy enough to fly your horse kite.

Jumper

A horse that participates in show jumping - There is no subjective scoring involved; the horse and rider team with the fastest time and the fewest faults wins.

Kimblewick

A type of bit.

Knacker

A person who disposes of sick or injured livestock animals.

Knee

The carpus (carpal joint) on a horse is commonly referred to as the "knee" which is only on the front.

Laminitis

Inflammation of the laminae of the hoof.

Latigo

Long strap on a saddletree of a western saddle to adjust the cinch.

Lead

1. Leading leg of the horse at the canter.
2. A line or rope attached to a halter and used to lead the animal.

Lead Rope

When his parents told him to find a stable job.

I'm not sure this is what they meant.

Lead Change
Horse changing from one lead leg to the other at the canter.

Leader
Horse(s) in a multiple hitch which are ahead of the pole or shafts.

Line-Back
Also called dorsal stripe - ribbon of darker color running along the back, stretching from the mane to the tail.

Live Foal Guarantee
Guarantee that a mare will have a living foal from breeding to a stallion.

Liverpool Bit
Adjustable curb bit used for horses in harnesses.

Livery Stable
Stable for boarding of horses.

Longeing
Longeing or lungeing is exercising and/or training horses on a line approximately 23 feet long.

STUBBORN?
You mean smarter than your training skills?

Long-Lining or Line Driving
Unlike lunging, long lining allows the trainer to have connection through both reins either to the bit or to a caveson.

Lope
Slow, relaxed three beat gait (a canter) seen in western horses.

Mare
Female horse older than three.

Markings
Refers to white markings on the horse's face, legs and body.

Martingale
Tack used to control the horse's head height - two most common types of martingale, the standing and the running.

Mechanical Hackamore
A hackamore is a bridle with no bit. A mechanical hackamore is a bitless bridle with shanks.

Martingale

Mule
Hybrid of a male donkey and a horse mare.

Nagsman
A man employed to ride and show horses especially in a sales ring.

Natural Cover
Breeding of horses through natural means without use of artificial insemination - also called "live cover".

Near Side
Left side of a horse - referring to the side on which a horse is mounted.

Neck Rein
Using the reins to touch the horse on the side of the horse's neck to turn and direct the horse.

Neigh or Whinny
Loud noise made by horse.

Nicker
Soft noise made by horses - a vibrating sound the horse makes with its mouth closed using the vocal cords.

Off Side
The right-hand side of a horse.

Maybe she's barn with it?

Maybe it's Neighbelline?

On The Bit

"On the bit", "behind the bit" and "above the bit" are terms used to describe a horse's contact with the bit. When "on the bit", the horse reaches for the contact with the poll as the highest point and the front of his face on or slightly in front of the vertical.

On The Buckle

Reins are buckled together at the ends so this means holding the reins very loose - "on the buckle".

Out Of

In breeding, the relationship of a horse to its dam.

Outlaw

An aggressive, unmanageable horse.

Pace

Gait of a horse - a two-beat, lateral gait in which the front and hind legs on the same side are moving forward at the same time.

Paddock

A fenced area for keeping horses.

Pair

Two horses in a side-by-side formation.

FOR SALE:
Blue Roan Gelding

Hancock bred, big
and strong, wears
a big shoe, needs
his teeth done,
not a kids horse...

Panic Snap
Quick-release snap for
cross ties and trailer ties -
If a horse panics, the snap
can be slid open with one
hand to free the horse.

Panic Snap

Parrot Mouth
A congenital
malformation of the upper
jaw where the incisor teeth protrude beyond the
lower jaw.

Pastern
The segment of the leg between the fetlock and the
coronary band.

Pedigree
The provable lineage of an animal.

Performance Class
A horse show class, either in harness or under saddle
- judged by performance of tasks.

Phenotype
The term phenotype refers to everything that we
can see about a being, from morphology and color
to behavior. The opposite, genotype, refers to the
being's genes and hereditary information.

When you miss that one goal and cost your team the game.

OR when you see a really cool ant!

Piebald
Colored splotches on a white background, primarily black splotches on a white background - The skin under the darker splotches may or may not be pigmented, the skin under the white background is not pigmented.

Pigroot
Bucking into a canter mostly caused by a rider's inability to let the horse go as the horse tries to make the transition - often a knee jerk reaction of the rider due to a fear of the horse rushing when they break into a canter.

Pigroot

Pinhooking
In terms of thoroughbred auctions, pinhooking yearlings describes the practice of buying yearling horses at auction or privately, overseeing their breaking and training and eventually re-selling them as race-ready two-year-olds in training. The same practice can be done with weanlings to resell as yearlings.

Place
Refers to finishing in a race, generally the second place out of the first three positions in some races Also refers to horse show awards.

Plug
Something inferior, useless, or defective, especially an old, wornout horse.

Points of a Horse
External anatomical notable structures of a horse, like crest, withers, shoulder, cannon, etc.

Pointing
Horses point one front limb forward when they experience pain in the rear part of the limb, especially the hoof. Pointing is more common in front limbs but a similar stance can be adopted with a hind limb.

Pole
A bar extending from the front of a vehicle, meant to be held between a pair of horses.

Poll
Part of the horse's head right between the ears - the occipital protrusion at the back of the skull.

Pony
A small horse breed which matures below 14.2 hands.

Posting to the Trot
To adapt to the rigors of horses traveling long distances at a trot, postillion riders adapted a method of rising and falling with the rhythm of the horse's gait and thus the name "posting" or "posting to the trot".

Prix St. Georges
The first level of international competitive dressage in FEI competition.

Produce
The off spring of a mare.

Pulling the Mane
The practice of removing longer hairs on the mane by pulling them out.

Purebred
A horse with breed registry verifiable by documented lineage.

Purse
The monetary incentive in any competitive horse event.

Putting To
The process of connecting a harnessed horse to a vehicle.

Quarter Horse
A North American horse breed - known for short bursts of intense speed and agility.

Goes to a Concert

Is the MANE Event

Quirt
A short whip associated with the Southwestern United States - It often has a braided leather lash.

Rearing
Rearing occurs when a horse "stands up" on its hind legs with the forelegs off the ground. Rearing may be linked to fright, aggression, excitement, disobedience, or pain. It is not uncommon to see stallions rearing in the wild when they fight, while striking at their opponent with their front legs. Mares are generally more likely to kick when acting in aggression, but may rear if they need to strike at a threat in front of them.

Red Speckled
Grey or roan horse with chestnut speckles on a predominantly white background.

Registration Papers
Verified documentation provided by a breed registry noting ownership and lineage.

Ridgling, Rig
Refers to a male horse that has a cryptorchid (undescended testicle).

Ring Sour
Undesired behavioral problems developed in a horse caused by competition burnout.

Rein

Straps, usually leather, attached as a pair to either side of a bit, used by a rider to direct the horse.

Roundup

The gathering of livestock - most often in the American West.

Saddle

Supportive structure for a rider or other load, fastened to an animal's back by a girth - The most common type is the equestrian saddle designed for a horse.

Saddle Blanket

Protective pad placed between the horse and saddle to protect the horse's back.

Saddle Pad

Pad shaped fully or partially to complement the outline of the saddle - placed underneath the saddle.

Saddle Seat

A form of English riding designed to set the rider farther back on the horse, for riding gaited horses and other breeds where high, flashy, action is encouraged.

My Face when...

they tell me their saddle fits every horse they put it on.

Riding side saddle, still better than walking.

Sand Pit
A sandy area specifically for horses to roll in after exercise, usually covered with deep sand.

Semi-Feral
Not truly feral, as they are privately owned and roam under common grazing rights belonging to their owners.

Shafts
A component of a horse-drawn vehicle consisting of a pair of rigid bars which connect to the front of a vehicle and run along the sides of the horse.

Show
Third place in a U.S. horse race - also refers to a bet that a horse will finish third or better.

Shying
The reaction of a horse to rapidly move away from an unfamiliar stimulus.

Side Saddle
Riding with both legs on the near side of the horse, as opposed to one leg on either side.

Sire
The father of a horse.

Smooth Mouth

Applies to a horse 12 years of age or older when all cups are gone and the grinding surface is smooth.

Snaffle Bit

A snaffle bit is the most common type of bit used while riding horses. It consists of a bit mouthpiece with a ring on either side and acts with direct pressure.

Snort

A loud sound made when the horse forces air out through the nostrils with the mouth shut.

Sound

Term used to describe a healthy horse.

Sour

Describing a horse with a poor demeanor and attitude in relation to being ridden.

Splints

Hard lumps, which are actually bony enlargements found on the side of the horse's leg between the knee and the fetlock joint, located where the splint bone runs down on either side of the cannon bone.

Sport Horse

A type of horse, rather than any particular breed -The term is usually applied to horses bred for the traditional Olympic equestrian sporting events of dressage, eventing, show jumping and combined driving; but the precise definition varies.

Stable

A structure built to house horses.

Stable Hand

A groom tasked with looking after the horses.

Stable Vices

Any negative behaviors relative to horses in confinement such as cribbing, weaving, wood chewing and wall-kicking.

Stagecoach

A public transport coach pulled by horses.

Stall

Individual horse enclosure within a stable building.

Stallion

A mature, uncastrated male horse.

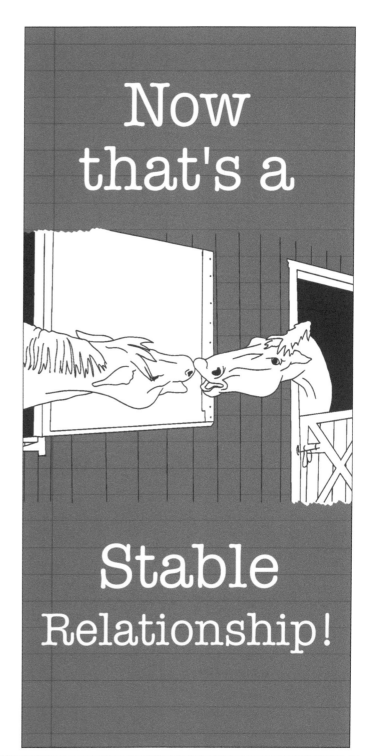

Now that's a

Stable Relationship!

Over heard at the barn:

"Today's riding lesson is No Stirrup themed, so tomorrow's to-do list will be No Standing themed."

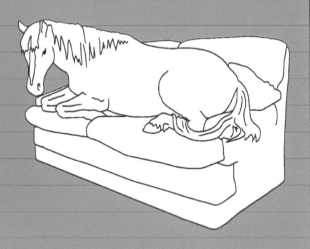

Star Mare
Thoroughbred broodmare who has successfully produced two or more winners in at least three of the eight most important and valuable races within the last six generations - in other breeds: a rating system that determines quality.

Stirrup
Paired frames, attached to the saddle, designed to hold the foot of a rider.

Stock Horse
A stock horse is a horse of a type that is well suited for working with livestock, particularly cattle. The related cow pony or cow horse is a historic phrase, still used colloquially today, referring to a particularly small agile cattle-herding horse.

Stock Saddle
Heavier style of saddle with secure seat, designed to help keep the rider seated.

Stride
Distance measured from the placement of one foot until the same foot hits the ground again.

String
Group of horses owned by one person - often each horse has a specific talent for use by the owner (cowboys choose a horse in their string for the use that day - herding, cutting etc.).

Stringhalt
A disorder marked by a jerking movement, higher than natural in either one or both hind legs.

Stud
Stallion - when made available for breeding to outside female animals are said to be "standing at stud".

Stud Book / Breed Registry
An accepted and established list of horses of a particular breed and their lineage.

Stump Knocker
Residual stumps after clearing forests that are hurdles for carriages.

Substance
Refers to the state of overall physical structure of a horse.

Suckling, Suckling Foal
An unweaned foal that is still nursing.

Sulky
A two-wheeled one person cart pulled by a single horse.

Non-Horse People:

"Omg! Look at the baby horse!"

Equestrians:
facepalm

Surcingle

Training equipment which goes around the barrel of the horse.

Tack

Refers to any equipment worn by a horse.

Tack Room

A location where tack is kept.

Tail-Female, Mare Line

Maternal ancestral line.

Tandem

Driving arrangement with horses in single file.

Team

Any of several configurations of more than one horse pulling a vehicle (draft horses 2 or more, light horses 4 or more).

Thoroughbred

Specific breed of horse, best known for racing.

Tie Stall

An enclosure in a stable, no larger than 6 feet wide by 10 feet long, designed to tie a horse.

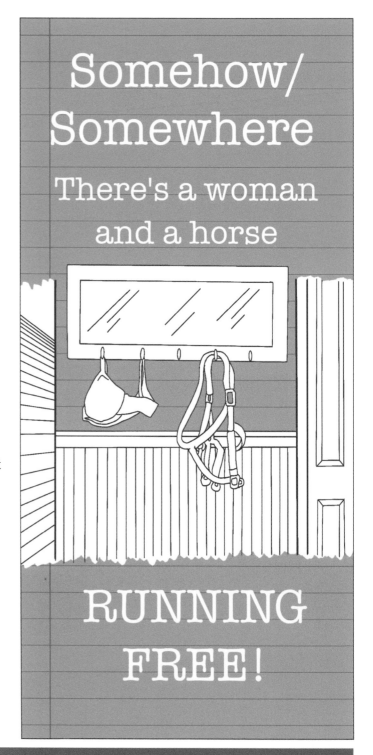

Somehow/ Somewhere

There's a woman and a horse

RUNNING FREE!

FABULOUS TROT!
And the horse is nice too.

Topline
Horse anatomy term referring to the area that runs from the poll to the dock.

Transition
The point in a horses stride when it changes gait.

Trap, Pony Trap
Light, often sporty, two-wheeled or sometimes four-wheeled horse or pony-drawn carriage, usually accommodating two to four persons in various seating arrangements, such as face-to-face or back-to-back.

Trap

Trot
A two-beat intermediate speed gait marked by diagonal hoof placement.

Twitch
A horse restraint involving the upper lip or ear, which calms the horse.

Unsound
A horse with significant health issues.

Vanner
Light draught work horse usually associated with the pulling a commercial vehicle - also called Gypsy Vanner horse.

Oh, your bank account is feeling stable? Here, let me stick my leg through this fence.

Veterinarian / Vet
Licensed Doctor of Veterinary Medicine (DVM) - person trained to provide medical care animals.

Wagon
Horse-drawn vehicle with four wheels made for hauling goods of various kinds, and/or for carrying people.

Walk
Four beat gait - slowest gait of a horse.

Warmblood
Middle weighted sporting horse - name derived from the cross of a hot blood horse and cold blood horse.

Weanling
A weaned foal, less than one year old.

Weaving
A stable vice, in which the horse repetitively shifts his weight and moves from side to side.

Western Show Riding
A competition using western style equipment to perform patterns which display skills in reining, trail and pleasure riding.

Wheeler
In a team of four or more - the horses closest to the vehicle. In a tandem - the rearmost of the two horses.

Whorl
A circular development of hairs and used as a means of identification.

Wild Horse
Horses that have no genetic evidence of domestication.

Xenophon
Greek cavalry officer 430 — 354 BC - historian and philosopher known for writing a manual on horsemanship describing humane methods for the training of horses.

Yearling
A horse from 12 to 24 months of age.

Zebroid
Hybrid off spring of a zebra crossed with a non-zebra equine.

WHAT'S IN A NAME?
Horse-related names

NAMES FOR GIRLS

Eowyn from literature means "horse joy" in Old English.

Epona is of Celtic Mythology and is derived from Gaulish epos meaning "horse".

Morgan is an American breed of horse.

Philippa is Old Greek origin. The meaning of Philippa is "lover of horses, friend of horses".

Pippa is a girl's name short for (or derived from) Philippa.

Rhiannon was the Welsh horse goddess, described as dressed in shining gold and riding a pale horse. "Rhiannon" was also made popular by the haunting song with the same name by Fleetwood Mac, sung by Stevie Nicks.

Rosalind means "gentle horse" and is derived from the Germanic elements hros "horse" and linde "soft, tender." A timeless, classic name, other popular variant forms include Rosaline, Rosalin, Rosalyn, Rosalynne, Roselyn, Roslyn, Rose, and Rosie.

Rosamund is used predominantly in English and its origin is Germanic. The name Rosamund means horse protector; rose of the world; pure rose.

MY NEW RIDER is COMING SOON

NAMES FOR BOYS

Arvan is Sanskrit and Old English. From Sanskrit roots, its meaning is horse.

Baylor means "horse trainer".

Colt is a young male horse. Colton and Coltrane are popular variants.

Horst is derived from Germanic origins. The name could be from the German element "horst" (meaning wood, wooded hill) or else from the Old Saxon "horsa". The name was first adopted by German speakers in the 15th century.

Howard is of Old Norse origin containing the elements ha (meaning "horse, high") and ward ("warden, guard"), suggesting a derivation from the job title of a warden.

Marshall is derived from a surname which denoted a person who was a marshal, shoe smith, or horse servant. Marshal derives originally from Germanic marah "horse" and scalc "servant."

Philip is derived from the Greek name Phillipos, which means "friend of horses" or "horse lover". Popular variant forms: Felipe, Felipo, Filippo, Phil, Philipp, Philippe, Philips, and Phillip.

Roan is a term to describe a horse's coat color pattern characterized by an even mixture of colored and white hairs on the horse's body. It's a variant of Rowan (Gaelic), and it means "little red-head." Roan Barbary was the name of favorite horse of King Richard II.

Rohon has its origins in the English-American language. The name Rohon means "from the horse country".

Ross derivations suggest the root word as the Old German "hros".

Roswell is of Old English origin. The name means "famous well; horse well".

Ryder is of English origin and means "knight", "mounted warrior", or "one who rides".

Stede is of English origin. Stede's meaning is "stud horse".

Stoddard is Old English. The meaning of Stoddard is "caretaker of the horses or oxen".

Tsin is of Native American origin. The name's meaning is "one who rides a horse".

Lightning Source UK Ltd.
Milton Keynes UK
UKHW051457120821
388718UK00002B/20